Misanthropes Rarely Procreate

Misanthropes Rarely Procreate

Poems by

John David Muth

Cover design by Shay Culligan

ISBN: 978-1-954353-67-1

Kelsay Books
502 South 1040 East, A-119
American Fork, Utah, 84003

For Nancy and Steven

Acknowledgments

Better Than Starbucks!: "Benadryl and Whiskey"

Misfit Magazine: "Father Under Glass," "My Chinese Name"

Rat's Ass Review: "Great Aunt Kate's Unsuccessful Accident"

Verse-Virtual: "Transcripts are Forever"

Contents

Part I

The Magical Orange

Black Soil Fertile

Great-grandmother Mary's parents
were old when she was born,
old in 1898 but middle-aged today.
They married her off at fifteen
to Phillip, a man twelve years her senior
in case they died earlier than expected.

Mary did her wifely duty
despite her youth and ignorance.
She was black soil fertile.
The first of six children came
just before the First World War.

Under five feet tall
Sicilian olive skin
sixteen-years-old,
she took her baby for long walks
to escape from her domestic chores.

Passersby would peek inside
the baby carriage
tell her she had a cute sister.
Mary would retort
perhaps embarrassed
or maybe defiantly
that the child was not her sister
but her daughter.

I imagine some of them thought
sixteen was too young
even in those days.
Mary admitted as much
to her three surviving children
many decades later.

Carmella

It was somewhere in Buffalo, New York,
sometime in the late 1920s
when my great aunt Carmella lay in bed,
ill with diphtheria.

The doctor informed my great-grandparents
there was no hope
said to make her comfortable
give her whatever she wanted to eat.

Great-grandfather Phillip
sat on his youngest daughter's bed
asked her in broken English:
Carmella, are you hungry?

Ten-years-old, with a raspy voice
Carmella looked up at her father.
Papa. I want capicola.
Phillip gave her what she wanted
preparing yet again
to lose another child.
She would be the third.

Sixty years later,
a cranky old woman
swore that the spice in the meat
dissolved the blockage in her throat
and thereby saved her life.

She lived to be almost eighty
loved to travel
always had money
and never had children.
I feared her as a child.
Now, she is my idol.

After the Diphtheria

A framed photo of my great uncle Anthony
sits on top of my bookcase,
blond and blue-eyed
an army hat tilted on his head.
I never knew him.
He was killed during World War II.

It is hard for me to imagine
the effect on my great-grandparents.
For eighteen years
they pushed a heavy cart
up a ridge pocked with potholes.
Every step was another day
of childhood sickness
and schoolyard fights
sprained ankles
and broken bones.
When they finally reached the top
and the eaglet was ready to fly
an earthquake erupted
he fell off the mountain.
The cart lay smashed
at the bottom of a canyon.

After the diphtheria
whooping cough
and measles,
a bayonet in the spine
and all that hard work
all that worry
ended with a white cross
somewhere in Luxembourg.

Great Aunt Kate's Unsuccessful Accident

Kate was almost 40 in the late 1950s,
pregnant with her third child.
The first was a boy,
eight-years-old,
who liked to shoot stray cats
with a homemade bow and arrow.
The second was a miscarriage at eight weeks.
She convinced herself
it would have been a boy.
The gender of the third
was not then known.
It was a mistake.

Three months before,
her husband Joe reached for her,
a night when he didn't reek of beer
or groan from nightmares
about Kassarine Pass
or Omaha Beach
and she let her contempt subside
did not turn her head away
as she often did
even when the room was black.

Standing at the head of the stairs
laundry basket in hand
she readied herself for a tumble
that might be blamed on weak ankles
or a spell of vertigo
so common in women of the time
and hoped for that sensation
a warm flow between her legs,
the contents of a cracked honey pot
left out in the sun.

The Magical Orange

I sit on the couch
in a friend's apartment
watch her toddler play
with lettered blocks.

A rubber ball rolls from the next room
toward the little girl.
She follows its journey
mesmerized.
It stops at her feet and she laughs.
Her mother then reveals herself
laughing in response.

A memory falls out
of an overflowing wastepaper basket:
something an aunt told me decades ago.
My great-grandfather Phillip
would toss an orange
through the front entrance of his house
when he returned from work each day.
His baby son Gino
would see the orange roll across the floor
and know his father was home.

That's all I know about Gino.
He didn't live very long.
It might have been
the 1918 Influenza Pandemic.
There's no one left who knows for sure.

Watching my friend coo to her daughter
I hope the child has a good life
and there's more to remember of her
a century from now
than a tiny fragment
of a story told third hand.

An Ode to Dr. Brydon

From the ramparts of Jalalabad
in 1842,
a speck on the horizon
grows larger.

A lone rider
slowly comes into view,
head cut open,
horse stumbling from dehydration.

This man,
a British surgeon
left Kabul the week before,
part of an army of thousands.
Everyone else was killed or captured.

Cold, starvation, and bullets
tried to keep him from his destination.
Was it more hardiness or luck
that determined his success?
Was there a creator who declared:
Let it be?

In 1971,
I set out on a perilous journey
watched all my comrades die
one by one
to reach my own Jalalabad,
I, the microscopic version of Dr. Brydon,

I, living proof
the birth control pill
is only 99% effective.

Part II

A Little Too Old for That

Two Years Is Cotton

We have been together now
for five years:
three years of dating,
two of marriage.
It's been relatively tranquil,
few arguments or disagreements
though she was disappointed
I did not buy her cotton
for our second anniversary.

In bachelor school, I never learned
every wedding year
requires a different material.
Emily runs through the list
memorized just before her first marriage:
10 years is tin
11 is steel
12 is silk.
The items get noticeably more expensive:
40 is a ruby
50 is gold
60 is a diamond.
My smile could be mistaken
as a pleasant acknowledgement.
It is really relief I will likely be dead
by the time we get to the gems.
This is an advantage of marrying late in life.

Admittedly, I'm looking forward
to anniversary three.
That one is leather.
Maybe I'll buy her a riding crop.

The Waitress Rolls Her Eyes and Walks Away

Our hostess takes us to a table,
the last one in the diner.
Next to us,
a father and mother gaze at their smartphones
while a toddler shrieks between them.
Its face is smeared
congealed blue.
Plate shards and corn kernels
surround the legs of its high chair.

Emily and I look at each other.
In our minds, we pick the parent
we would use as a shield
if a maniac came in shooting.

I'm glad she dislikes children
and inconsiderate parents
almost as much as I do
though I sometimes worry
she'll change her mind.
I'll be trying to chase a child
with my future artificial hip
praying for an artery to burst
and deliver me from middle-age fatherhood.

Another Semester for a College Advisor

I crouch in a trench,
a World War I soldier,
dirty and unshaven
helmet dented by shrapnel
waiting for the signal.

The whistle blows
and I go over the top
alone
running across no man's land
running to retirement:
a speck beyond
the minefields and barbed wire.

Thousands of students shoot at me.
At first, they miss quite often
as it's difficult to aim
a bolt action rifle or Maxim Machine Gun
when one is texting.

Their parents get angry
take the guns from their children's hands
and shoot at me themselves.
Red holes patter across my limbs and torso.
I cannot fire back.
My orders prohibit me from defending myself.

I tumble into a shell crater
flesh and uniform shredded.
A grenade falls into my lap,
brown and hissing,
followed by another
and another.
I smile just before the flash.

The shriek of my clock radio
jolts me awake.
I am still alive on the first day of classes.
It is almost disappointing.

A Little Too Old for That

7:00 a.m. at the Farrington Diner
still half-asleep
the sound of sucking attracts my attention.

A young woman nurses her son
at the table next to mine.
She sees me gazing,
aggressively stares back
as if to ask if I had a problem.

I would like to respond
her child looks old enough
for first grade by now.
If she keeps enabling him like that,
the only breasts he'll ever suck
will be hers.

Instead, I look down at my breakfast,
two eggs, sunny side up
reach for the coffee creamer
and sigh with near certainty
he'll be one of my students
in a little over a decade.

Transcripts are Forever

A student comes into my office
barely groomed
hair reaching in waves
toward the ceiling lights.
The smell of dirty clothes and cigarettes
settles in my nose.

He tells me he was just diagnosed with ADHD
so the one F and two D's
he received over the last three semesters
should be erased from his transcripts.
The classes with C's or better can remain.

Smirking at his arrogance,
I inform him erasing transcript grades
is like aborting a child
that has already been born.
Unfortunately, it is not possible.
His ADHD did not seem to be an issue
for the dozen other classes
he passed satisfactorily.

He gets up to leave,
calls me a dick under his breath.
I ignore his insult and stare at my phone
wondering how long it will take
for his mother to call.

Bread Causes Highway Hypnosis

The Adirondack Northway
is quiet north of Lake George,
few rest stops and not many cars.

Emily commandeers the radio
whenever we go on a trip,
loves music from the 1970s,
Todd Rundgren and Graham Parsons,
musicians barely known
to younger generations.
She passed out
halfway through *America's* greatest hits.

Bread is the next band on her playlist,
somnambulist kings
and the first song is their crown jewel:
    If a picture paints a thousand words...
An invisible hand tries to close my eyes.
The surrounding countryside is so peaceful.
    If a man could be two places at one time...
It is getting rather difficult
to stay between these long, white lines.
    If the world should stop revolving
    spinning slowly down to die...
Keeping my eyes fixed on the road
I try to find a song
from *Deep Purple* or *Led Zeppelin*
so I don't fall asleep
launch us off of this mountain.
    Then you and I would simply fly away...

Lunch on a Lake George Cruise

Try not to look
directly at the other happy couples.
They may want to talk
ask us questions about where we're from
the attractions we've seen
whether we like the chicken piccata.

We are on vacation to rest and reconnect.
Everyone else is an obstacle
to walk or drive around,
background characters in a movie
who mouth a few inaudible words
while quickly walking off-screen.

The loud one in the backward baseball cap
is looking over at us.
He might want to start a conversation
share some of that corny humor
that seems to make the other couples laugh.

Put your steak knife to my throat
look angry
angrier.
Recall the day I said
your favorite blue dress
made you look like a librarian
in a low-budget horror movie.
That's the angry we need.
Lament aloud that no one's bled out
face down in this lake
since the French and Indian War.
He'll never want to speak to us.

She Wasn't Taught Very Well

Shopping for shampoo and soap
at my local CVS,
I see a girl
maybe twelve-years-old
unattended
in the hair care section.
She takes a brush from the rack
and runs it through her long, blond hair.

An oblivious voice
calls out to her.
She puts the hairbrush back.
Fronds of corn silk
dangle from the bristles,
sway as she runs to rejoin her mother.

I suddenly remember
I also need to buy condoms.

It Was Supposed to be a Nice Evening

She whispers,
teasing the hair in my ears
with her breath
tells me all the things
she wants to do to me tonight.

This is the fifth anniversary of our first date,
a night out at an upscale restaurant,
the overture to an opera
where the lovers die from mutual exhaustion.

A young couple enters the dining room,
probably BMW SUV drivers.
A pale-faced boy walks between them
holding their hands.

They're here to celebrate
little Zachary's graduation
from the first grade-
his ground-breaking research in napping,
his innate ability
to aim correctly when he pees.

His mother rattles off
his food allergies to the waiter
and many other ailments unrelated to food.
The boy loudly asks for chicken nuggets
in a place that serves
boar shank and quail eggs.

His parents converse
about whether to enroll him
into Aztec pottery making
or no-contact sabre fencing
while the child endlessly repeats
a greeting in Mandarin Chinese.

Father Under Glass

A priest once asked me
if I believed in angels
the kingdom of heaven
the resurrection of the body.

I told him sure.
My sister insisted I lie.
It was the only way to be
my niece's godfather.

Fifteen years later,
I am less spiritual guide
and more father under glass.
If Glenda's parents
murder each other
over child support payments,
I will be the one to take care of her
pay for her college education
criticize her taste in men
walk her down the aisle
help her fill out divorce papers.
I'll do the best I can.
She is the one person under twenty-five
who doesn't annoy me.

She wants to play the xylophone
in the high school marching band
and I am reassured
even if tragedy strikes her parents
I'll have more than enough time
to save up for a wedding.

Charmin Rose and Kleenex Dove

I walk into the bathroom
after a visit from Glenda,
notice a toilet paper rose
crowning the roll.

A dove made out of tissues
perches on the towel rack.

On the threshold of sixteen
she is still a sweet girl,
innocent and trusting
able to see something pretty
in the mundane tools of excretion.

My sister was already dating
losers-in-training at her age
and I found as much comfort
on a psychiatrist's couch
as I did in my own bed.

I put the rose where it won't get crushed,
hoping dysfunction
might have skipped a generation
and she'll be the kind of happy
we were both too cynical to be.

Our First Christening

It took two trains and two taxis,
a mile walk in the hot August sun
to get from central New Jersey
to this Catholic Church in Babylon, Long Island.
Emily's girlfriend
is having her first child christened here.

Long Island is the hernia scar
of the mid-Atlantic,
cut by a surgeon whose wife left him
the evening before the operation.
I come here only when necessary.

By the time we take our seats
the first of six couples is already with the priest.
A lipless young woman
with a spray tan
chews gum over the baptismal font
as a slightly older man
with gelled hair and sleeve tattoos
looks at the ceiling.
Either the priest is using sulfuric acid
or the infant is pure evil
as a shriek ricochets off the walls
the moment the water touches his forehead.
Wait till you have to pay a mortgage, kid.

An hour later, the ceremony is done
and all six babies are wailing uncontrollably.
I look at my wife
head bowed
lips pursed
gritting her teeth.
She hates loud noises.

Part III

A Moment to Ourselves

Please Stop Posting These

It would not be summer
without having to see
a plethora of women
in their third trimester
posting pictures of themselves
at the beach
in very tight bathing suits.

It makes me think of Oedipus
sitting blind and in agony
after stabbing his eyes.
He never had to see
tan bulges straining
against multi-colored patterns,
herniated umbilici
ready to pop like champagne corks.
I almost envy him.

First Night in Houston

There is something in the weather
that invites disintegration.

Palpitations from over-salted food
bring insomnia.

A pain in my left eye socket
will not go away
no matter how many aspirin I take.

I chew on hotel wallpaper
waiting for the sun.

Our first morning brings pity
for the first astronauts
forced to live here
before air conditioning was common
when there was even less to do.

I would curse any location
that has me longing
for the skyline of Newark, New Jersey.

Emily assures me
Austin is a far more interesting place.

Visit on a Custody Weekend

We sit on a sofa chair
in a three-story Houston townhouse
holding hands as if terrified.

Her brother Dave
lies on the living room couch,
head propped up with cushions
holes in his socks:
hard-jawed with tri-color hair,
light brown with blond and gray streaks.

Five children by two different mothers
roll around his outstretched legs
chase each other around the kitchen table.
Screams echo through the hallways and staircases.

Unperturbed, he plays with his phone
waiting for ex-wife number three
to drop off child six
so we can all go out for dinner.

Emily tries to distract herself
by watching TV.
I look out of a window
briefly imagine what it might be like
to have so many children,
see myself gray and balding
hanging from the walnut tree outside
overdue bills stuffed into every pocket
while angry women
with frosted hair and too-tight jeans
whack my dangling corpse with sticks
like a piñata with no more candy to disgorge.

Looking Forward to No Future

We sit around a long table
in a barbeque restaurant:
Emily and Dave,
all six of his children.

It's hard to hear above
the noise his children make
as they argue with each other.
Most of the other customers
hardly seem to notice.
They have loud children of their own.

Dave asks us when we are having kids.
We tell him never.
Surprised, he asks us why.
I look at the little zombies
sitting closely next to me
grunting, screeching, crying
eating chicken and ribs
with red-stained hands and mouths.

He does not understand my subtlety
and starts to flirt with our waitress.
Her name is Dalene.
She is a single mother of three.
This piques his interest even more.
He asks for her number.
I ask her for water.
She puts a finger to her lips.

Emily looks at him incredulously.
He says children give a man purpose.
There is no future without them.

I agree with his last statement
just as son number two
(I think his name is Jason)
wipes his greasy hand on my sleeve.

Benadryl and Whiskey

We stand for hours
in the baggage check section
silent and forlorn
like ancient Egyptian slaves
sealed into a pharaoh's tomb
waiting to die from starvation.

Sometimes, there is movement,
the shuffling of feet
a stanchion rattling
from the careless brush of a purse.
The self check-in kiosks are all down.
Slowly moving airport employees
sip Benadryl and whiskey
from large metal cups
as they scribble signatures
on boarding passes
stifle laughs as the elderly
try to lift their suitcases onto the scales.

I give my boarding pass
to a frowning man
balding and bespectacled
put my luggage on the scale.
He tells me there is an extra charge
for bags over 50 pounds.
The scale reads 36.5 pounds
until he puts his foot on the pressure plate
and the weight jumps to 51.3.
When I open my mouth to protest
he says it is entirely possible
they will find a firearm
hidden in my shaving kit.

A Moment to Ourselves

An aging airbus
soars high above the Texas sky,
Spiritual Airlines
flight 13666.
My wife did not want a layover
and this was the only nonstop flight
from Houston to Newark.

The passengers begin to murmur
from the sound of thunder rumbling.
Cabin windows slowly turn gray.
Emotional support animals
bark and squeal from the turbulence.
Their owners are comparatively calm
but do nothing to quiet them.

The rain becomes heavy
making it hard to see outside my window.
I imagine myself
as a pre-*Star Trek* William Shatner
on an episode of the *Twilight Zone*
watching a pug-nosed creature
in a shag carpet jump suit
pull one of the engines apart.

I don't think I'd mind a crash
if we were the only survivors.
Maybe we'd land on a remote mountaintop
or deep within an old growth forest.
The solitude might be refreshing
as we get so little time
to ourselves these days.

A Halloween Scare

They bang on my storm door loudly
and I walk reluctantly down the stairs
holding an orange bowl.

I should have pretended to be out
turned off all the lights
locked the door
but Emily thought we should be good neighbors
bought a large bag of chocolate bars.
She then went to bed early
complaining of a headache.

The costumes this year are pretty crappy:
little clowns in smeared make-up,
Disney princesses I never heard of,
kids in plain clothes and plastic masks
who just want candy.

A teenager in a blue suit
and a black rubber pompadour
holds out a pillow case,
frowns when I only put in one bar.
His mother approaches with arms folded
tells me he is President Reagan.

A Pleasant Little Thanksgiving

It's quiet this Thanksgiving,
no twenty-pound turkey this year
no need to bring out the folding table.
It's just dad, Emily and me,
a bit subdued but not unhappy.

My sister is working
a double shift at the hospital.
Glenda is at a restaurant
with her father
his new girlfriend
and her two young daughters.

This is her father's third relationship
since the divorce six years ago.
Each woman has had young children.
Each time, the relationship ended
largely because of the children.
They couldn't adjust
to a new man in their lives.
Glenda is cautious as a result.
She won't get too close to anyone new.

After dinner, I send her a video
of dad sleeping on the couch,
snoring with his mouth wide open.
She responds with a text:
I can do better than that,
and sends a video of her own father
arguing with his girlfriend
while her youngest daughter
lies on the floor
shrieking from a tantrum.

I Could Eat That

They gather at the corner:
my neighbors with their dogs
talking and laughing
while their animals bark,
entangle themselves in their leashes.

I have overheard their conversations
enough times to guess their content:
Jewels the Rottweiler
ate a whole bag of *Twizzlers*
when Dan got up to take a leak.
Rocky the Pit Bull
took a shit on Mary's wool rug
to protest a new toy he didn't like.

It's cold outside.
A light dusting of snow
covers the grass and sidewalks.
Before the yapping distracted me,
I was reading an account
of the siege of Leningrad,
how the starving citizens
exchanged their dogs and cats
with their neighbors
so they didn't have to eat their own pets.

I look at Emily's dog,
watch the foamy drool
fall on my newly cleaned floor,
notice the new teeth marks
on the legs of my dining room table.

A survivor from the book
said that dog meat tastes a bit like mutton.

I like mutton.

Attempting Consolation

Emily lies on our bed.
Desolation seeps from her pores
like oil in a long-deserted car.

The dog had to be put down yesterday.
He had arthritis,
intestinal problems.
I try to cheer her up,
suggest a trip to a winery
or a walk through her favorite nature preserve.
She tells me another time.

He was her dog, not mine.
I never got along with him.
The giant, whiny Saint Bernard
failed out of three obedience schools.
Still, I must respect her grief.
He was her baby,
the closest thing to a baby she will have,
a symbol of domesticity
when she lived in New York City,
a source of comfort through her divorce,
the death of her grandparents.

My family never had pets
so I can understand
but cannot fully feel her loss.

Maybe one day,
after a bottle of Merlot or two,
I might suggest we get a dog:

a cat-sized breed
that doesn't bark
and never pees in the house.
Till then, maybe I'll buy her some fish

or a very nice potted plant.

Twelve Cards a' Burning

We hate getting Christmas cards
from friends and relatives
as we have no desire to learn
how much their children have grown
or see how well they can fake a smile
in front of a fireplace.
To know everyone is doing well
is adequate for us.
In some cases, even that isn't important.

Twelve cards came in the mail this holiday.
A cousin from Georgia is the most noteworthy.
He is wearing a baseball cap and a Santa outfit
cradling an AK-47
while his wife and five children sit at his feet.
The caption reads:
Santa fights to keep Christ in Christmas.

I remember that AK-47.
He showed it to me
during a visit several years ago,
referred to it as his baby,
told me with pride
it could shoot 30 socialists without reloading.
I requested a three-minute head start
as a family courtesy,
but he didn't get the joke.

His will be the last card
we ignite on the Yule log
Christmas morning.

He Assumed Incorrectly

During a family Christmas party
an obstetrician cousin
I see once every three or four years
heard Emily and I were childless
and assumed it was not by choice.
He recommended in-vitro fertilization
as a viable option.
Adoption was also a good last resort.

I asked him if someone had a predisposition
to lung cancer
but managed to avoid it well into middle age
why would he celebrate
by buying a carton of unfiltered cigarettes?

He walked away without a word.

The Apocalypse Excuse

When people ask us why
we haven't started a family,
we might tell them
the prospect of ecological disaster prevents us
and visions of the future
bring us sleepless nights:
giant islands of floating plastic
the yellow-brown haze of a city sun
desiccated wheat rotting in a field
forest fires and hurricanes
my vintage *Star Wars* action figures
submerged under sewer-tainted floodwater.

We might include radioactive shrouds
over nuclear reactors
exploding electrical transformers
creating frozen statue families
huddled around dead TVs
in pitch-black, snow-covered houses.
For our progressive friends,
we often add corporate exploitation
the decline of retirement pensions
unaffordable health insurance
rising poverty
economic inequality
lingering racism
religious bigotry
growing authoritarian executive authority.

If we really want to confound our inquisitors,
we tell them we don't like children very much.

Part IV

We Could Be Trees

Sperm Attack

They race toward their destination,
millions of middle-aged sperm cells
like a fleet of Model-T Fords
attacking the Death Star.

Engines whine and die suddenly,
some drive endlessly in circles
others stop to ask for directions
but there is no one to ask.

The vagina
is a hostile environment for sperm.
The vagina
is a hostile environment for most men.
It was for Brad,
that's why he didn't date much
and didn't marry until his 40s.

One cell speeds ahead of the others.
It hears a voice:
Luke, use some force.
Fertilize that petrified egg
so future dad can get some sleep.

Luke honks his horn
puts the pedal to the floor
suffers a blowout
crashes and explodes

necessitating yet another trip
to the fertility clinic.

Abstaining from Multiplication

Emily's friend is pregnant at 41.
After many attempts
she calls it a joyful surprise
but I imagine a bolt of lightning
a carelessly tossed cigarette
that ignites a forest fire
burns and grows
becomes a conflagration
that necessitates evacuation.

I would not be a father at 47.
My own mother died at 67.
My father is 72,
a survivor of three cancers.
Death runs its fingers through his hair
punches him in the stomach
to remind him of his debt.

Religion says it's holy to multiply
our culture says it's expected we multiply
society says we're strange
if we do not multiply
the economy says
it's worth the heavy debt to multiply.

Only the environment
applauds us in the empty theater.
We take a bow,
a small but growing troupe
who do not want
the picket-fenced house,

the ones unwilling to sacrifice
what's left of our vigor
and what's left of our time.

My Chinese Name

Emily and her pregnant girlfriend
discuss possible names
for her unborn daughter.
Her favorite is *piao liang.*
It means *beautiful* in Mandarin.
I roll my eyes at the pretension.
Neither she nor her husband is Chinese.

An ex-girlfriend gave me a Chinese name.
We dated just before I met Emily.
She was pretty and fun
but very traditional,
wanted a baby right away.

She was thirty-five.
Her parents were pressuring her
to marry and have children,
an ancient expectation
that often brings unhappiness.

I came to realize I did not want children
and told her when she asked me
where our relationship was going.

Her usual stoicism shattered.
She called me a deceiver
a betrayer.
Her last word came as a slap:
hun dan.
A friend of mine later told me
it meant *asshole.*

No one else knows my Chinese name,
only she and I.
It was deservedly bestowed
but never proudly held.

Men Die First

The winter cold
creeps through cracks
in the windows and door,
sinks heavily into the couch
reaches for us
as we lie by the fireplace.

I stare into the flames
while Emily sleeps,
orange-skinned:
a Van Gogh portrait
with tangled blond hair
and light green eyes.

This morning, we discussed
what to do with our mortal remains.

Emily insisted
she wanted to die first
so she wouldn't be alone.
I did not remind her
women live longer than men.
It was not worth an argument
and there are exceptions.

I lean closer to the warmth
trying not to remember
my father's request
we visit the mausoleum this weekend
where my mother sleeps
undisturbed by pestilence
or any other earthly care.

We Could be Trees

I don't want to be buried in a cemetery
knowing you will complain
about the chill of the underground
or how your casket only has one pillow.
You might even ask me
to climb outside
and tell trespassing teenagers
to stop fornicating on our tombstone.

Cremation is better
but we can't share the same urn.
Visitors might notice
the top popped off
my ashes scattered around the base.
Much like our bed
you will inevitably take
far more space than you need.

There is a way to be buried
with the seed of a tree.
Our remains become fertilizer
to propel its growth.
Can you see us now
as a fully grown oak or elm
bursting green every spring
for decades?

If they plant us close enough
we might be able to touch,
maybe even rub branches,
slowly and intimately
on those long, moonless autumn nights,
after the squirrels have gone to sleep
of course.

Cello Sonata for a Childless Couple

We will live our lives together,
not ostentatiously
like a late Romantic symphony
or a double concerto
where each instrument
fights for center stage.

We are more similar
to a sonata.
You are the cello,
soaring and soulful
sincere and empathetic.
I am the piano,
versatile and grounded
wistful and contemplative.

Do not lament
we'll never be a string quartet
quintet for winds
septet for brass.
The size of the ensemble
pales to the strength
of the melody.

Our tiny ensemble
will make many melodies,
melodies with different tempos
different textures,
most of them beautiful
some of them dissonant
but always returning
to the home key,
harmonious until
the final notes of the coda.

Dreaming of 2075

I had a dream it was 2075.
Glenda was in her 70s.
She was sitting on a bed
running her fingers
through the hair of a teenage girl.

Between sobs
the girl stammered
no one would ask her to the prom
because she was 6'2" with a big nose.

Glenda smiled,
told her granddaughter about me,
how I was tall with a large nose,
how hard it was for me to find dates
when I was young.

The girl asked her grandmother
what happened to me.
She responded I married at forty-five
never had children
and died when I was seventy-eight,
had a heart attack
during a *Lord of the Rings* convention
dressed as Gandalf.

My grand-niece started to wail loudly.
Glenda tried to assure her
I died where and when I wanted
but her efforts were in vain.

Glenda quietly left the room
remembering her inability to console
was something she learned from me.

About the Author

John David Muth was born and raised in central New Jersey. He has been an academic advisor at Rutgers University over twenty years. In addition to writing, he enjoys hiking, road trips, and volunteering for environmental causes in his spare time. He is a member of the U.S. 1 Poet's Cooperative. His work has appeared in such journals as *Better Than Starbucks!, Verse-Virtual,* and *U.S. 1 Worksheets.* He is the author of five collections of poetry: *A Love for Lavender Dragons* (Aldrich Press, 2016), *Inevitable Carbon* (Aldrich Press, 2017), *Odysseus in Absaroka* (Aldrich Press, 2018), *Reassure the Phoenix* (Aldrich Press, 2019), and *Dreams of a Viking Wedding* (Aldrich Press, 2020).

www.ingramcontent.com/pod-product-compliance
Lightning Source LLC
Chambersburg PA
CBHW031151090426
42738CB00008B/1290